So Much To Say

A Book of Quotes

by
Craig Stewart

Published by Craig Stewart

Impeccable Works, LLC

www.CraigTheWriterStewart.com

Cover Design by: Byron Holly

ISBN-13:9780692969038

Dedication

This book is dedicated to those I don't know who supported my gift by pushing my dream forward. Because you took a chance on my work by spending your hard-earned money, I'm here. Because you were selfless, you shared me with your friends, family, even posted me and/or my work on your social media, I'm here. This one's for you. Thanks for giving "the kid" a chance. I'm forever grateful.

Table of Contents

Encouragement

A Whisper of Hope to Your Spirit

Single mothers raising little boys are in the unique position of raising their boys to become the men they were never able to find – faithful, honest, committed.
(Craig TheWriter Stewart)

Your imagination is God's proof of what's possible in your life.
(Craig TheWriter Stewart)

You never really have it all figured out. Keep climbing.
(Craig TheWriter Stewart)

Sometimes you just need courage to let go.
(Craig TheWriter Stewart)

Heartbreak has the potential to teach you to appreciate love when it appears again.
(Craig TheWriter Stewart)

Faith requires discipline.
(Craig TheWriter Stewart)

God will connect you with those you need to be connected with when you need to be connected with them.
(Craig TheWriter Stewart)

It's your journey. It's your dream. It's your responsibility.
(Craig TheWriter Stewart)

When we give up on what was, we can finally enjoy
what is. Let go.
(Craig TheWriter Stewart)

Being hungry for it makes you better at whatever it is
that you do.
(Craig TheWriter Stewart)

Relationships recycle. The person you're best suited
for could be in the wrong relationship while being
prepared for you.
(Craig TheWriter Stewart)

It's easier to give up than to keep going.
(Craig TheWriter Stewart)

Never regret the time, effort, energy, affection or emotion you invested in a relationship. You're better because of it.
(Craig TheWriter Stewart)

Have patience with the process. Greatness takes time.
(Craig TheWriter Stewart)

People can see the calling on your life, even when your life seems to take a detour.
(Craig TheWriter Stewart)

You're still on course.
(Craig TheWriter Stewart)

Your strength inspires someone. They're watching and waiting to see how you pull through.
(Craig TheWriter Stewart)

Fear will cost you your dreams.
(Craig TheWriter Stewart)

Timing is everything. Sometimes you have to put it down and come back to it later.
(Craig TheWriter Stewart)

Everything can change for the better in an instant.
(Craig TheWriter Stewart)

Stop trying to understand everything.
        (Craig TheWriter Stewart)

Fear will make you lose hope.
        (Craig TheWriter Stewart)

It all has purpose, even if you can't see it yet.
        (Craig TheWriter Stewart)

Stop pushing so hard. Allow the dream to breathe.
        (Craig TheWriter Stewart)

Not everyone will understand your sacrifice.
(Craig TheWriter Stewart)

Dreams require all your energy.
(Craig TheWriter Stewart)

Don't force anything. There's a time to push, a time to pull, and a time to yield.
(Craig TheWriter Stewart)

You're right where you need to be. Pay attention to the lessons.
(Craig TheWriter Stewart)

Keep quiet about what you're doing. Your friends and family will project their fear about *your* dream on you…
                    (Craig TheWriter Stewart)

Everyone has an idea about what you should do with your life, but are clueless about their own.
                    (Craig TheWriter Stewart)

If you can see it, you can be it. If you can touch it, you can have it.
                    (Craig TheWriter Stewart)

Instant gratification will never fill you up. You'll always be hungry for more.
                    (Craig TheWriter Stewart)

Carve out the life you want for yourself.
(Craig TheWriter Stewart)

God is always speaking. We're just not always listening.
(Craig TheWriter Stewart)

Sharing your dreams with the wrong people will cost you time and energy explaining and defending your ideas.
(Craig TheWriter Stewart)

Listen to your inner spirit even when you doubt.
(Craig TheWriter Stewart)

Most can handle good. It's *great* that intimidates.
   (Craig TheWriter Stewart)

Oftentimes, depression is broken faith.
   (Craig TheWriter Stewart)

Never stop dreaming. Never stop believing. Never
stop wishing. Never stop hoping. Most importantly,
never stop praying.
   (Craig TheWriter Stewart)

For every step of faith that you take for yourself,
God will take three for you.
   (Craig TheWriter Stewart)

Wait. Your turn will come.
(Craig TheWriter Stewart)

Stop making excuses. That's fear talking.
(Craig TheWriter Stewart)

When you're great they have no choice but to notice you.
(Craig TheWriter Stewart)

Abandon the idea that you're supposed to be someplace other than where you are right now.
(Craig TheWriter Stewart)

Decide that giving up is not an option.
(Craig TheWriter Stewart)

There's something really sweet about gradual, but we want what we want now – and yesterday.
(Craig TheWriter Stewart)

Most don't understand the sacrifices a dreamer makes for the dream.
(Craig TheWriter Stewart)

Most can't handle different. Be different anyway. It makes you special.
(Craig TheWriter Stewart)

Following your dream requires you to trust that everything will work out in the end.
(Craig TheWriter Stewart)

Craig Stewart

Relationships

Romantic, Interpersonal, Familial, Platonic

Who knows anything when it comes to love, but there's a point at which enough suddenly becomes too little and there's no other choice but to let go.
(Craig TheWriter Stewart)

Consistency *ain't* common.
(Craig TheWriter Stewart)

Compromise for a relationship isn't a problem — settling is.
(Craig TheWriter Stewart)

There's a point in every parent's life that they must admit to themselves that they weren't perfect, and there were some things they could've done differently.
(Craig TheWriter Stewart)

Even after the dust settles and the relationship is over,
there's collateral emotional damage.
(Craig TheWriter Stewart)

There's a fine line between what a parent can give a
child and what a child wants for themselves.
(Craig TheWriter Stewart)

Love doesn't wait for us to organize our lives. It will
pass you by.
(Craig TheWriter Stewart)

Trust is built or broken by consistent behavior.
(Craig TheWriter Stewart)

Be strong enough to walk away without second guessing or looking back.
(Craig TheWriter Stewart)

Sometimes the consequence of being a person of quality, with standards, is being single. Never lower your bar. The *one* will match your morals, values and standards.
(Craig TheWriter Stewart)

Love me enough to see past my past.
(Craig TheWriter Stewart)

I'm single because I'm unwilling to go along with things that some want to get away with.
(Craig TheWriter Stewart)

Love humbles us.
>(Craig TheWriter Stewart)

Communication is attractive.
>(Craig TheWriter Stewart)

I love love.
>(Craig TheWriter Stewart)

Trust isn't limited to cheating. It extends beyond loyalty & integrity, and reaches towards good judgment.
>(Craig TheWriter Stewart)

Love me enough to see past my past.
(Craig TheWriter Stewart)

Sometimes a person isn't quite ready to be the person
they say they can be for you.
(Craig TheWriter Stewart)

I'm not afraid of being in love. I'm afraid of being
there alone.
(Craig TheWriter Stewart)

It takes the right kind of love to grow you out of your
bullshit.
(Craig TheWriter Stewart)

Insecurities can be dangerous to love.
(Craig TheWriter Stewart)

Don't let your ego keep you in a situation that isn't good to you or for you.
(Craig TheWriter Stewart)

Desperation isn't attractive.
(Craig TheWriter Stewart)

Stop selling the idea of yourself to someone who doesn't see your value. If they can't see your worth, move on.
(Craig TheWriter Stewart)

There's nothing you can say to make me trust you.
Your actions will teach me to.
(Craig TheWriter Stewart)

Love happens as organically as friendships.
(Craig TheWriter Stewart)

Stop campaigning for someone to be with you.
(Craig TheWriter Stewart)

Communication is a rhythm. It's a dance, but it's a
dance that has to be learned over time.
(Craig TheWriter Stewart)

Most miss their chance at love because they believe they have the rest of their life to plan for it.
(Craig TheWriter Stewart)

Focus less on what they say about you, and more on what you know to be true about yourself.
(Craig TheWriter Stewart)

There are things you know to be true about yourself that you can never say out loud. Otherwise, you run the risk of looking and sounding both crazy and cocky.
(Craig TheWriter Stewart)

Social media is the cause of death for many relationships, and the reason many others never get off the ground.
(Craig TheWriter Stewart)

Don't confuse interest with thirst.
> (Craig TheWriter Stewart)

Many are in relationships that are already over. They just haven't ended yet.
> (Craig TheWriter Stewart)

If I can't be honest with you, I can't be your friend.
> (Craig TheWriter Stewart)

Friendships aren't always reciprocal, but there should be balance.
> (Craig TheWriter Stewart)

If you think being a friend means I can never tell you no, then you have the meaning of friendship all wrong.

(Craig TheWriter Stewart)

Sometimes the people we grow apart from are family, and that's ok too.

(Craig TheWriter Stewart)

A man is only interested if you're interesting.

(Craig TheWriter Stewart)

A long relationship doesn't always mean a healthy relationship.

(Craig TheWriter Stewart)

It's easier to walk away than to stay and fight for it.
(Craig TheWriter Stewart)

If I can't trust you, I'll never love you.
(Craig TheWriter Stewart)

Just because the relationship looks live from the
outside doesn't mean it's not dead on the inside.
(Craig TheWriter Stewart)

It takes more energy and effort to hold your heart
back than to give it. Just save a piece for yourself.
(Craig TheWriter Stewart)

Admitting it's over is the first step to healing.
(Craig TheWriter Stewart)

Family can be as toxic as cancer, leaving us no other option but to cut it off.
(Craig TheWriter Stewart)

I'm interested in sharing my life with someone, but that doesn't mean I want to give my life away.
(Craig TheWriter Stewart)

Your insecurities sponsor more stories than you'd care to admit.
(Craig TheWriter Stewart)

There's power in letting go.
(Craig TheWriter Stewart)

Fear will cost you love.
(Craig TheWriter Stewart)

Never shrink for the sake of a relationship.
(Craig TheWriter Stewart)

Everyone claims to be ready for marriage until the date is set.
(Craig TheWriter Stewart)

Allow love to breathe. Otherwise, you'll smother it to death.

(Craig TheWriter Stewart)

It's ok to have standards. But having a "type" keeps you single.

(Craig TheWriter Stewart)

Know when someone isn't ready for you and all that you bring to the table. Sometimes your light is simply too bright, and that's ok. Be patient. Wait on greatness.

(Craig TheWriter Stewart)

When it comes to dating, I can compete with the best of them from the door, but no one can compete with history.

(Craig TheWriter Stewart)

Never confuse compromise with settling.
(Craig TheWriter Stewart)

Effort communicates your interest.
(Craig TheWriter Stewart)

Love without losing yourself.
(Craig TheWriter Stewart)

You're never required to have a tangible reason to end a relationship or to walk away. Your instincts alone are enough.
(Craig TheWriter Stewart)

Some are more selective about who they follow on social media than about who they sleep with.
(Craig TheWriter Stewart)

Securing a date is the easy part. Getting to the relationship is another story.
(Craig TheWriter Stewart)

You'll never have to chase love. It happens without force.
(Craig TheWriter Stewart)

Inconsistency is unattractive. It's tantamount to being a habitual liar.
(Craig TheWriter Stewart)

Love will never keep you from your dreams.
(Craig TheWriter Stewart)

Spend more time listening, and less time defending.
(Craig TheWriter Stewart)

I refuse to become inconsistent just because consistency has become uncommon.
(Craig TheWriter Stewart)

A person can fall in love with your accomplishments, but never fall in love with you.
(Craig TheWriter Stewart)

If your end goal is to be in a relationship, don't waste time with people who can't handle the responsibility of loving you.

(Craig TheWriter Stewart)

You can't make him ready, but you can let him go.

(Craig TheWriter Stewart)

They walk away when they know they're not enough for you.

(Craig TheWriter Stewart)

Love is easy. Relationships are the challenge.

(Craig TheWriter Stewart)

Confusion in your personal life can cause
confusion in your professional life.
(Craig TheWriter Stewart)

Good guys don't finish last. We just move on to the
ones who will appreciate us.
(Craig TheWriter Stewart)

You can't be scared to love. Otherwise you'll leave
your partner starving emotionally.
(Craig TheWriter Stewart)

My last relationship didn't work, but it didn't scar
me. It made me better for the next.
(Craig TheWriter Stewart)

You don't have to compromise the joy of being
yourself for the sake of being with someone — ever.
(Craig TheWriter Stewart)

We can become so accustomed to dysfunction that
it's impossible to recognize healthy when it finally
shows up in our life.
(Craig TheWriter Stewart)

Fear will try to convince you that you have to take the
first offer that comes your way — you don't.
(Craig TheWriter Stewart)

At some point it begins to feel like a game, and
though you try to ignore the signs you realize the only
way to stop playing is to simply walk away
(Craig TheWriter Stewart)

I can't invest my time where there's no interest.
(Craig TheWriter Stewart)

Your instincts will tell you everything you need to
know about a person. Just don't confuse fear with
instincts.
(Craig TheWriter Stewart)

Leave if you don't feel valued.
(Craig TheWriter Stewart)

Your love should be earned—not given away.
(Craig TheWriter Stewart)

Don't allow your partner's insecurities to keep you from growing towards your dreams.

(Craig TheWriter Stewart)

Relationships don't repair insecurities, cure emptiness, or heal loneliness.

(Craig TheWriter Stewart)

A relationship can "grow" you, but it transcends when it heals you—when you heal each other.

(Craig TheWriter Stewart)

Your insecurities sponsor stories that aren't true.

(Craig TheWriter Stewart)

There's a fine line between attempting to understand someone's behavior and making excuses for them.
(Craig TheWriter Stewart)

The secret sauce of any great relationship is pairing with someone who wants what you want, at the time that you want it.
(Craig TheWriter Stewart)

I love to see love. It reminds me that it's possible for all of us.
(Craig TheWriter Stewart)

Stop making poor decisions out of loneliness.
(Craig TheWriter Stewart)

We all say we're looking for the same things; love, honesty, trust, and consistency. If we're all looking for the same things, why then haven't we found each other?

(Craig TheWriter Stewart)

Push past fear to love.

(Craig TheWriter Stewart)

Delete the number or you'll abuse the number.

(Craig TheWriter Stewart)

A b-r-e-a-k up stings, even when you initiated it.

(Craig TheWriter Stewart)

Just because you're ready, doesn't mean everyone
who crosses your path is.
(Craig TheWriter Stewart)

It's one thing to be ready for sex. Intimacy is another
conversation.
(Craig TheWriter Stewart)

All love isn't intended to be a forever kind of love.
(Craig TheWriter Stewart)

You can't be afraid to walk away. You just may be
walking towards possibility.
(Craig TheWriter Stewart)

Craig Stewart

Just because it didn't last doesn't mean it wasn't love at its best. Stop discounting it.
(Craig TheWriter Stewart)

Sometimes our ability to be monogamous expires before the relationship ends.
(Craig TheWriter Stewart)

The goal of dating, for me, is love.
(Craig TheWriter Stewart)

If it isn't love, I don't want it.
(Craig TheWriter Stewart)

I've broken some hearts and my heart has been
broken, so I've learned from both. What I know for
sure is that we've all been someone's disappointment.
(Craig TheWriter Stewart)

Pay attention to the one paying attention to you.
(Craig TheWriter Stewart)

Vulnerability is attractive.
(Craig TheWriter Stewart)

You can't be so afraid of starting over that you stay
instead.
(Craig TheWriter Stewart)

Craig Stewart

Be sure you can handle the responsibility of love
before asking for a relationship.
(Craig TheWriter Stewart)

Sometimes we get so used to dysfunction that we
don't know how to operate without it — so we stay.
(Craig TheWriter Stewart)

Love is for everyone. Relationships are for the
mature.
(Craig TheWriter Stewart)

Your feelings are your feelings, even if you never tell.
(Craig TheWriter Stewart)

Wisdom

A Glimmer of Light in Darkness

Happiness doesn't just happen. It's a series of good decisions.
(Craig TheWriter Stewart)

Confidence isn't loud — insecurity is.
(Craig TheWriter Stewart)

If you're more interested in praise over constructive criticism, then you're not really interested in growing.
(Craig TheWriter Stewart)

Rock bottom is a part of life. Keep living.
(Craig TheWriter Stewart)

Trust life. Trust that it gives you everything you need, good or bad. Nothing is happening to you. It all happens for you — for your benefit.
(Craig TheWriter Stewart)

Only a fool believes that if he continues to *pretend* he can become.
(Craig TheWriter Stewart)

We're different in every moment. We see things in a new way each time we go back to it, whatever it is – a song, movie, love. Whatever.
(Craig TheWriter Stewart)

Prayer isn't magic. Get to work. Do your part.
(Craig TheWriter Stewart)

A flower that blooms in darkness can survive anything.
(Craig TheWriter Stewart)

Everything happens as it should. It's all designed to grow you. Even the stuff that hurts…
(Craig TheWriter Stewart)

Unknowingly, we tuck things away on a mental shelf, and we're not reminded of them until something triggers us to remember we locked it away.
(Craig TheWriter Stewart)

Use the resources you have now. Focus on those and not the ones you believe you need.
(Craig TheWriter Stewart)

Ego helps and hurts us.
(Craig TheWriter Stewart)

People will try to penalize you for not being the person you once were.
(Craig TheWriter Stewart)

Indecision is a decision.
(Craig TheWriter Stewart)

Being skilled at "robbing Peter to pay Paul" doesn't mean you're good with money.
(Craig TheWriter Stewart)

Envy is the first step to jealousy.
(Craig TheWriter Stewart)

The things they accuse you of are often the things they're guilty of.
(Craig TheWriter Stewart)

Sometimes you have to step away from a situation to appreciate its value, and to see all you've learned.
(Craig TheWriter Stewart)

Success is inspiring without knowing you're inspiring.
(Craig TheWriter Stewart)

Even when you anticipate the worst from a situation, it doesn't change how much it hurts when it actually happens.
(Craig TheWriter Stewart)

People like to see you rise up to have something to aspire to, and tear down.
(Craig TheWriter Stewart)

If it's always easier for you to pick up and walk away, you probably have commitment issues.
(Craig TheWriter Stewart)

Gossip travels faster than good news.
(Craig TheWriter Stewart)

Just because a person doesn't help in the way we want them to doesn't mean they haven't helped.
(Craig TheWriter Stewart)

Envy is fear that God won't be as generous with your blessings.
(Craig TheWriter Stewart)

It's impossible to be in love with someone you pity.
(Craig TheWriter Stewart)

There's a fine line between being relatable and being phony.
(Craig TheWriter Stewart)

We don't always do better simply because we know better.
>   (Craig TheWriter Stewart)

Sometimes you have to say it out loud to begin healing.
>   (Craig TheWriter Stewart)

When did you stop trusting? Find the answer to that and you'll find the key to your brokenness.
>   (Craig TheWriter Stewart)

Don't expect someone to be honest with you if there will only be penalties for doing so.
>   (Craig TheWriter Stewart)

Dysfunction is some people's normal.
(Craig TheWriter Stewart)

Keep it to yourself so the decision is truly yours, not the thoughts and opinions of the people around you.
(Craig TheWriter Stewart)

What do you believe after you separate what you've been taught from what you know for yourself?
(Craig TheWriter Stewart)

Oftentimes, confidence is confused with cockiness, but it's usually insecurity confusing the two.
(Craig TheWriter Stewart)

Live without apology.
      (Craig TheWriter Stewart)

Everyone says they're ready for love — until it shows up.
      (Craig TheWriter Stewart)

Conversation and confrontation aren't the same.
      (Craig TheWriter Stewart)

Integrity is a necessity for greatness.
      (Craig TheWriter Stewart)

Whatever you chase will always elude you – success, money, even love.

(Craig TheWriter Stewart)

Confidence isn't loud. It's subtle, but noticeable. It doesn't beg or scream for attention.

(Craig TheWriter Stewart)

Trust your instincts. They're always right.

(Craig TheWriter Stewart)

There's a bit of contradiction in all of us.

(Craig TheWriter Stewart)

Everyone who congratulates you didn't celebrate you in the beginning.
(Craig TheWriter Stewart)

There's a fine line between attempting to understand someone's behavior and making excuses for them. Be clear, they are two different things.
(Craig TheWriter Stewart)

We can summon people, things and events to our life.
(Craig TheWriter Stewart)

A key to life? Knowing when to push and when to pull.
(Craig TheWriter Stewart)

Craig Stewart

Don't confuse fear with instincts.
(Craig TheWriter Stewart)

You've either adapted to the dysfunction or you've
learned to crave it.
(Craig TheWriter Stewart)

Famous doesn't mean confident.
(Craig TheWriter Stewart)

The beauty of patterns is that we can break them once
we're honest with ourselves about them.
(Craig TheWriter Stewart)

Sometimes we're too close to the light to see its potential and promise.
(Craig TheWriter Stewart)

It takes years to brew greatness.
(Craig TheWriter Stewart)

The best get-back is saying nothing at all.
(Craig TheWriter Stewart)

A person can't argue without your participation.
(Craig TheWriter Stewart)

A weak mind sees your celebration of self as boasting or bragging. Leave them be. That's not your business.
(Craig TheWriter Stewart)

Some of the most prideful people are homeless. Ask for what you need.
(Craig TheWriter Stewart)

Gratitude is easy. Finding the balance between gratitude and wanting more is tough.
(Craig TheWriter Stewart)

When you take away all that you've learned, all that you've been taught and conditioned to believe about life and the world, what do you really know?
(Craig TheWriter Stewart)

Friendship isn't determined by time or years in. It's quantified by the value someone brings into your life.
(Craig TheWriter Stewart)

No longer do I allow fear to dictate my choices. I've retired from that busy work.
(Craig TheWriter Stewart)

There's something to be said for humility and forgiveness. One can't exist without the other.
(Craig TheWriter Stewart)

We're always of the belief that someplace else is better than where we are. It isn't.
(Craig TheWriter Stewart)

Just because you only live once doesn't mean you live recklessly.

(Craig TheWriter Stewart)

Take your ego out of it. What's left?

(Craig TheWriter Stewart)

There's a point at which humility can feel like a broken spirit.

(Craig TheWriter Stewart)

No one lies to you more than you lie to yourself.

(Craig TheWriter Stewart)

Learn the art of sitting still. It's necessary. That's when God is speaking loudest.
>   (Craig TheWriter Stewart)

Looks may get you through the door. Confidence will keep your seat at the table.
>   (Craig TheWriter Stewart)

People need people. Don't ever think you can make it in this world alone.
>   (Craig TheWriter Stewart)

Folks say they want the real thing 'til the real thing shows up.
>   (Craig TheWriter Stewart)

People aren't perfect.
> (Craig TheWriter Stewart)

Sometimes people push you away because they haven't the slightest clue what to do with all you offer.
> (Craig TheWriter Stewart)

If you're not ready to grow, you're not ready for love.
> (Craig TheWriter Stewart)

Love isn't petty, people are.
> (Craig TheWriter Stewart)

Your light may scare people away. Doesn't mean you stop shining. The real one won't be intimidated. He'll grab a pair of shades.
(Craig TheWriter Stewart)

There's a fine line between what you can control, and what's out of your control. Govern yourself accordingly.
(Craig TheWriter Stewart)

When you bless other people, God has no choice but to bless you. It's like a boomerang that has to come back.
(Craig TheWriter Stewart)

Don't be so literal that you miss the message beneath the obvious.
(Craig TheWriter Stewart)

Don't allow ambition to get the best of you. It'll convince you to take unnecessary risks.
(Craig TheWriter Stewart)

God rewards obedience and discipline.
(Craig TheWriter Stewart)

God grades us on a different scale than man.
(Craig TheWriter Stewart)

The moment we begin negotiating our nevers and compromising our standards is the moment we begin living in our nevers.
(Craig TheWriter Stewart)

You can remember the story any way you choose, but
the story happened the way it happened.
(Craig TheWriter Stewart)

Take the lessons. Leave the baggage.
(Craig TheWriter Stewart)

Sometimes we have to admit that we are the problem.
It can't always be everyone else, especially since we
are the common denominator.
(Craig TheWriter Stewart)

There's a fine line between celebrating one's success
and bragging about it.
(Craig TheWriter Stewart)

Sometimes the answer is to sit back, do nothing and
wait for God to move.
(Craig TheWriter Stewart)

Craig Stewart

Also available by Craig Stewart:

Words Never Spoken, a memoir

*One Thing for Certain, Two Things for Sure: a memoir
continued*

www.CraigTheWriterStewart.com